SEACLIFF

SEACLIFF

poems

CATE LYCURGUS

DURHAM, NC

SEACLIFF

Library of Congress Cataloging-in-Publication Data

Names: Lycurgus, Catherine author
Title: Seacliff : poems / Cate Lycurgus.
Other titles: Seacliff (Compilation)
Identifiers: LCCN 2024062318 |
ISBN 9781949344653 paperback
Subjects: LCGFT: Poetry
Classification: LCC PS3612.Y348 S43 2025 |
DDC 811/.6--dc23/eng/20250211
LC record available at https://lccn.loc.gov/2024062318

Published in the United States of America

Cover art: John Frederick Kensett, *Nahant* (1850)
Book design: Spock and Associates

Published by
BULL CITY PRESS
1217 Odyssey Drive
Durham, NC 27713
www.BullCityPress.com

TABLE OF CONTENTS

SEACLIFF

DELIVERANCE

All along the shore, waves spread froth fingers
purling as they reach. They don't quite
reach before receding, don't quite
recede before being trundled
up in another attempt. *Everything's coming right at you*,
they tell me, when what they really mean is
don't stand so far back. I watch one race
to sud sand clean—no matter
how close—the surge can't sweep the jelly back
before rushing in with another. Come
as far as it can touch, in the final
instant of hush—the orb
scuds away, opaque. What follows is only the slow-
seethe into a darkened-down beach. No
scrying, no crying—there are
no exquisite exits.
You can fail this relentless every day of your life.
And the tide never turn for you re-
turning might have to
suffice

TO SEE IT

All year I had asked
for a sign. Day out,
night in, every thought
dead-ended in such
suit. Before you could see
the surf—hear it, even—:
the crush of eucalyptus
came, soon their cobble of blue
pods with x-ed out
notches afoot. The crash
of water never stopped
not for you for
nothing. Insistent
the only question was—:
how many earshots
back. I stood so far,
each wave dropped
with the tiniest cymbal-
kiss—& leaned in
for it, but with eyes
shut—how to be
sure? & what if
everything is a sign—:
the windshield cracked

clear across, trailing
like a gentle horizon,
the horizon that rose
to match it? What
of the song foretelling
loss come on every
station at once, then
the bridge crossed
to make it, make it
happen? By some hand-
writing on the wall—all
fragments now—a complete
clause may surface, spell out
how to move. Play/
pause. I stopped
at the market, booth
after booth with prices
scrawled in thick
script over cardboard—:
3/$1, $2.50/lb a sign
& a sign & a sign the world
is here for the biting
into. The buying. __X__
here—, you must
decide

SKYLINE-TO-THE-SEA

There was a time we knew with certainty
what we would go and do. We called it
landing, we saw it *promised*, and dipped

our noses toward the bay, readied
our wheels above the waves' pacific
commas, bright-cresting delays—

and we trusted the ground
to reveal itself for our touching down
at the last second, never questioning

our own deaths. How tenuous they'd be.
This peninsula-city has no graves left,
buries dead in unknown places. Unfazed,

we embraced gravity, made our way
down the coast's arm to where you lay,
and took twenty questions to ascertain

your latitudes of ache. Head shaking, tube
raking along your parched throat—we can't
screen agonies closest to us—

where yeast has colonized the tongue
in a crust preventing speech. No bottle
brush tree can brush it off, nor we,

the need to have direction, be some
remedy—the dog has a blazon of burrs
on her chest, and we go home to pull

them off, find the fruit-of-the-month
sunk to counters, its scales a maze of rot.
We hold the knife as we hold

our lives: to the basket of pineapples,
not having cut one before. We twist
a crown, kitchen drowns in its manna

smell and slicing the scales we go for the core,
mangle it with our stubborn torque,
mostly throw them away. It's knives

we use for shredding and to do the spreading,
too. We stroke your hand all afternoon—
ambrosia that we're making; these days

we stomach canned fruit.

SEACLIFF

Since the break is all there is
to hear
I have to stop
listening over, to some high-
pitched patina
of voices
when what beats bedrock
is the only
sound one needs
to seek to not run
out of breath I pause
at the end of the path
on the wall
there's a brass
hand to high-five—
everyone does—no reason
but to celebrate—:
you went all the way
to say you did, show no stone-
wall can block
elation—,

that surf tries, cannot quite
catch you with icy-
frothed fingers' reach
despite the spray dampening
flyaways round your face
escaped from a hood's
drawstring—closed,
you cannot see but sense
to your right, the crest's surge
& slap every time
it builds but will not take you
out of strength kelp says
don't stop & grows on—on
you could yell
& no one hear—that loud,
so—no surprise
shoulders tense every time
it's one-one thousand
two, unloosed, ready if not
sundered then, for the chest's
giddy-up, headlong—
            into the light
                        that I love

The light I love has held out
on me—: socked-in mornings I flip-flop
atop the mattress, hip to hip
to keep either ball & socket from sinking
so low, & deeper than sleep—
where I'll pledge my heartbeat's loitering
only if the gray un-numbs,
is taken up by hills' canopies—*I can* I chant
& know I can't, not a chance
to stand on my own, let alone bench-press
the vault or hold, in a quaking
plank. Atop picnic tables people do, whole
minutes with waves so near
the spume blows in with ripe perfume
of rock dove; oh, I melt
for them, the undeterred—like my mamma
who sets the pot of coffee
even nights I am away *in case*, she says
which maybe means
there is another version of sky
depending on what we do, or we're dependent
on the doing. Along the promenade,
rangers thrust push brooms,
mound sand at the rail before a final sweep
& thud—like clumps

of brown sugar to the container, though
there's no containing glass-
grit nightly travels on, lays its fine coat
down. Till what was solid
ground before, shifts with whim of wind—
only breath holds the dust of me
up. Redundant then, to powder my face
when I covet sheen
wherever it seeps through
it isn't enough—to flip the hourglass, watch
as our spate passes, taupe &
it mostly feels this way, although
each broken grain gives back
the light crystalline & intact—what god
promised more than that

I need the reminder
every day, every day

I need the reminder
I'm married to this
world, relentless—:

to keep a narrative mind-
set not a toy drone's
range away from

see how the living-
room rug abuts stairs

down to the threshold
where road elbows round
the field interrupts

itself revising to cliff, bit-by-
drizzle, a little more
with each onshore squall

come to annul
my view of combers

below they throw
themselves down hard
ashore, so sure

of demise, of re-
combining forever
I wish I were half as sure

of anything
but my need to mind

the break daily—: how
steep the fall, the fog
between this awe

this terror

A bulb has changed
somewhere in the sky—I don't
like it, can't be
choosy—they say
everything changes,
but I wake beneath the same
ceiling. Beige watermark
arced as parenthesis
toward the pane,
the thought of day
still open. Statistically,
this is the first half
of life, though what will begin
has begun. & where
is the ocean's birthplace?
Most times, I can't tell
if it wants in or out—
the knocks sound cold, then
far off, take all footprints
with no effort, my mug
finds yesterday's stain;
the paper, a depression
in the path where brackish
pools blur all news
beyond salvage & in any case,

it was a gospel
I needed. Back in school
math daunted me—:
when stuck, teachers said *move*
to the next, assuming next
would be easier. I assume
nothing but that I will need
a coat. The key—: to not
pause at slate overhead,
its constant tease of no
rain, no sun break either
one would punctuate
the flat spanned platinum
ahead, marbled godwits
do their best, come up
empty is a type of set.
The flock disbands
far over water—a chasm
in cloud lets rafters
through; they poke
the surface, rucked & bright
& some comfort: a scaffold
strong & true, sea a-
luster—that there is light
elsewhere, even if not
for you

Never stop—the truck
does—barely—
at the sign & barrels
ahead—: a southwest swell,
dark infill of under-
sky, beyond the bodega
the drive-in past
power lines of cypress
trees RVs parked—
en route I can't speed
fast enough, take stairs
down to beach double-
time pitches me to my knees—
spring, neap, may tide me
over, but—I'm never over
their pull—is gravity
a weak force? What
would strong drive me
                              to do—

Not every morning but most mornings, late
I rise in a fog, languidly pulled

toward the esplanade where I run—not fast
not slow but dutiful, & south as far

as one can go—& note the surf—how close
or detached: there lustrous, here crumbled—

then swerve from strollers, pigeons' iridescent
necks—green blurred violet—rising violent past

all accommodations I make, make
no difference—flocks ascend regardless

of weather I am within it—: stubborn
cloud cover & no other option but beating it

back toward the pier with pylons
like apparitions, like all underpinnings—: part

ghost. & what to say to the naigo tree—drained
by thrips but holding on—in this landscape

there have been many ends of the world
as one knows it—there have been many

ends curl & drop—leaves or waves, unto a beach
we cannot see—this—the incessant mercy

Dear dune lupine, eucalyptus,
abalone holding on—along
the elbowed crook of bay,
cliff high, shelf
deep, constantly—beyond me: how
you fling bright banners
to the wind, extend
the hospitality
of shade without
throwing it, even with
the grounds to do so as silt-
stone erodes—to see
the diver come for you—
insides lined with nacre—but
luster *nonetheless*
sounds wild & antique—this late age
when all are less
commonplace—: to be born
neck deep in grief, I forget
to look. Which might be my gravest
admission—: letting the grim
roll in. Rather than toeing
names in sand, pacing end-to-
ending back where they've washed
out only partly, the naming

helps—Lu, Cal, Al—who else,
but particular yous, to lose?
We've known the answer
long as we've known death
as just one unit of distance; sin,
really our refusal to see
the rule—its sliding scale—
& the need to break it anyway
we can, at whatever
price. So dears—I will call you
all my life
            is your life—

All along Seacliff Drive: cars parked bumper
to bumper. Summer or pea soup, noon, quick

dusks—when the loneliest star comes to hug
the horizon—it's never without a crowd

for pictures, kisses, fifth period smoke
breaks; absolute best place to snarf the burrito,

play your song on repeat . . . maybe not so loud
as to drown out surf that brings you to tears—

not debt, prognoses, sheer exhaustion, but
surf, & the cement ship, now foundered below.

How its split level houses a squabble of gulls
soaring in sherbets of day blazoned down—

tangerine, pink, russet, then navy—where
only dark pleather waves crawl beneath

all fades—& no one tires of vanishing, but will
watch till there's nothing left to watch, throb

at the precipice till—hear: pounding persist
with its *yes*—I'd idle all night for this

Because I have to keep moving, I go
for the water. It has to keep moving

too close! a mother shrieks into a wind
so desperate for sound, it sucks

alarm straight from the mouth
where the creek gives up its name

a swoop of pelicans swerves overhead
beyond a red flag—which falters,

so strung out, there's no predicting
if the kite will lift or immolate—: one more

apprentice to the light. Once more. Cirrus
like bones of a prehistoric fish score

the sky opposite—before sun unrolls
its carpet of shine, the gleam is hundreds

of camera flashes capturing retreat—
like paparazzi, I know who to watch

as the runner lays down, beginning where-
ever I stand & on, to the end

of the earth. To sea—here, blinded by it
always—there is no other way
to live

There was no other way:

to live
days without
expectation for

anything can drift
-wood that clenched
incoherent sand-

stone too will lose
insistence, no use
palming

what you used to
see, naigo's
no longer tree

(candelabra
kayak coffee-
table) sea

will do this fling
& weathering
of hope

truncated, with
no object, no
objection

when the swell
sweeps in-
transitive so never

settled, never not cast
beyond sight
a splinter is one

of infinite shards
impossible
to remove, ignore

each step
what it was
you prayed for

DEAR LORD IF THERE IS GOOD IN STORE FOR ME

to find if sea stars lurk
by urchins spined and whole lives pool
beneath the noise of surf I'm poised
for tenderness through turquoise prod some tentacles
to glom on God, please send a tide
to sweep the brine
high time or if it's not then just some numb
to tide me over or
to shore me up its touch can take
me in as venom floods you've done
well with hide and seek of sink
holes I am sinking fast and tucking in as hermit crabs
but past hermitage I want to step
out into sun to scintillate for waves
to come and spray I pray
to hunker down tight enough to outlast un-
certainty of ever seeing
ships come in
the ice plant spreads across the cliffs
don't let me turn cold, the waves
are in and out relentless sea anemones
know no wilt and flower on
good was here all along
the enemy
was me

DEAR K,

Today I just couldn't stand. Every time a swell came up behind
me—even the long, gracious breaks—I'd clamber up only
to plummet. Into a mat of kelp no board's tail fin could hope
to cut. Russet & yards of it, soft as velvet, catching me in its drift.
I'm not one to resist embrace but—does the living ever take
you under? Blue on blue at great remove, up close it's blue
on green. You say from diagnosis to gone, seventy-six days
with your wife Dora; 11,601 suns rose on my wishing for the end
of paralysis, for my daddy to get up & walk, shit, just swallow
on his own—& he never could, ultimately—you too know
of many ways to be spectacle or stuck outside the lineup, never
your turn for a break, nor mine—what good does comparison
do? *Which would you rather*, Daddy asked once, *to be beheaded, or*
burnt at the stake? Didn't wait on his grin for me to weigh this—
a hot steak's better than a cold chop! & I have two wetsuits on
since it won't take Arctic swells, since 11° C will paralyze me
nonetheless, you've been frozen out most your life—how
did you—I can't stop shivering anger,—toss the boa
over your shoulder, remain pacific, when made to sit back
of the church for your own sweet Dora's service, with you
the only one who had immersed yourself in hers. Mamma
& I sat front row for his, no rail to grab, & everyone watching
us gasp in the wake—what to do with hands turned fins, finished,
but—are we ever? With him, her, it might not show, but I can't un-

learn the motions—K, which ones are you going through? Still
I turn on his prism light, set twice the cups of coffee, pour sludge
to the drain. They say to never look down nor back—only to shore
since single-minded carrying on will keep you on your feet. That it did,
once—: nearly miraculous as skating atop the waves. Set after set
greets me with spray, forced as shook champagne. So hard
to catch a swell, pop up, stay—much as I want to, in his stead remain,
I'm six feet deep in brine in muck impossible to lose & my leash
might be the snarl that saves. Not off, but tossed round my neck
the olive feathers gleam. I stroke them. Flounce
                    my boa at you, hope it buoys—as you do, me—

PROFLIGATE

A storm & the guard rails—:
gone. Along the strand

postholes slosh & well
with kelp, then empty—what

sentries remain say
have at it & ocean rolls in

with clap after clap—spray
like uncorked champagne

to endless applause—
for the pier, once a half mile

out, flicked like toothpicks
to the deep. But pampas

grass plastered against
the cliff whistles its same

flat key—could be last year,
year before, scores from now—:

no sign of the pit
rimmed with driftwood

where my first lust & I
bucked on sand in tandem

with surf & none but ghost
embers to witness—see

how you turn once, or
the earth does, round the sun

of another autumn closing
in the door of the fridge, fig

preserves wait, crystallized
in old knife divots, jar

still clean at the rim where I ran
my finger to steal some sweet

must be boiled reduced sealed
to keep that way after all

heat flees; what's abandoned
remains unseen in the farthest

corner somehow, same
how through the squall,

cypress screened the house
walled with windows

until the tree's rough cut
like a bad buzz at the nape

cast blotched shade
below the chin forever is

my weakness—: teeth
at the neck & I'll cave—wave

upon wave bites the scarp
this season, even the lot

is awash with foam & day-
trippers stalled to watch

fall swells breach
pavement, reach tires, rock

windshields more
than you wanted the pane

to hold you wanted
there to be none

to shatter—for all holding
back to expire, no difference,

inner or outer—:
how I want to be wholly
                                        slathered

THERE TOGETHER IS ENOUGH

Always I want the ridge. Neither sky nor
surf, instead—: wind-brushed fescue

lying flat for me to walk its part. A buck
bugles, distant but my rut is lorn &

mainly well worn in its quiet. Crests
like snails curl in on the right, ripped leather

ocean sheer to the left & a mind unable
to reconcile—I lick salt from the chap

of my lips, press up the peninsula's knuckle
—behind me—: not a soul. Ahead

tule elk lounge in sedge, like dozens
of bronzed corn dogs. With wide-set gazes

that throw off my hood for the creature
within. Appraising. What courses inside

all the time, in chambers where I'll never
stand—I want to canter closer, click

my ankle bones & whistle—: tell me,
who you see? Shooter marble

eyes know more than all the books
I'll ever read—those supermoon

pupils turn from mine, which narrow
in glare even as I learn myself

to look. Deep, one can sense the herd
pound; wind, shift; needlegrass chafe

as it converts light back into being—how
plain—: our sounding hour, receding—

NOT THE SONG BUT THE SOURCE

What chimes in me is not the point
of course it is
easy to get caught up when the land
breeze leaves every
night, withdrawing its cool touch,
then—how else attest
to sovereignty? More often no word
is the word
to relay; still, when hung so close
the suggestion
of wind sets lopped pipes atremble,
what else am I
good for—hollow, unmoved—waiting
for some excuse

GIVEN NAMES

Who could cling to the myth of accretion when arrived, like we have, at this
precipice? Where cypress once flanked makeshift steps now tumbled

unto sea, we have to keep back to see the system break, wild spray kick up
& anoint the rock as it takes Purisima with. Sandstone sanded down

to sand, only half what it was—the remainder shoring roots that will also
go—: where what it is is its undoing. We understood, with time; not only

would the outcrop cleave, sea pink drop off the shoulder, verge unshore
itself from street; but that we would lose all standing. All that remains of ours,

& the stint when it seemed dominion & redoubt could coexist, has
retreated—: quarter mile back, the Bliss Point lighthouse blinks, pointless,

into the blinding day. As though its pulse might lure ships in, hold strong
surf at bay. Below, riprap does its best—hauled & heaped against the face—

but steady friction reshapes. At the edge of the world, we sang in the round
with gulls & killdeer, an Airbus coursing overhead—combusting last millennia's

fens—none overlapping our cries. For belonging. Longing. To sustain
what we couldn't save, our throats graveled, choked, so we gulped from green

longnecks tossed to shatter; that shards would one day return to us, softened,
somehow mattered. How many filled a jar was anyone's guess; each hunk

confirmed how oceans can take up what's treacherous, render it smooth; yet
one was never enough—we needed proof after proof. That this was not

remarkable: to be wrecked beyond use, past all recognition & still worth
scooping
up. We who were A Part of All We Had Touched. We who were Apart
From Nothing.

SURFERS

The best recognize
when it's time—:
to stand, they greet
the horizon prone
—the only way
to begin—so far out
any contour could be
a wave, or just bird,
buoy, trick
of light, flattening
surfacing dark again against
the future's false line
which they try to read
regardless, sets scroll
over sea like a rough-
iced cake crumbling
with cross-shore gusts
boards jounce & slap
hard to trust a tide
change, wind shift, but
closed-out can't last
forever *not yours, not yours*
is a sort of hope held
fast they swing around,

start to rise ahead
of spray, ease off if crest-
fallen, still—
who doesn't love
legs that can lift
from beneath, to ride
the peel of a merciless
break, barreling on
to shore? Unsure
what builds at their backs
none can look
for what will carry
forth since where
you want to go
always ends
in crash transposed
back to wave—: my goodbye
has been so long
in motion

REPARATION

Amos 5:24

I wake & I can't even. *Level up*, the sea
confirms, urges me, like a swim bladder, to rise—
knock sand from my eyes, sleep from my kicks—how does it
look to hit the ground running, not be run aground—:
the man with his wine-dark glaze who grabs for bootstraps
as I pass newts flattened to their own endangered
silhouettes on asphalt &, whose fault? the coast-blown
pillar of smoke, creeping Jenny mowed down while crouched
beneath her desk—I want to lift the lid & tuck
her, her hopes inside beside the loose-leaf, torn sheets
I can't toss aside, unsee—, mourning has me lop-
sided, I plod the sloped shore, unsure how to be
impartial. When in parts. Beach glass breaks it smooth, how
in the dream, my ease isn't even a part &
shattered, only the start

ACKNOWLEDGMENTS

Many thanks to the editors of the following journals where these poems appeared, sometimes in earlier forms:

The Adroit Journal	"Skyline-to-the-Sea"
The Cortland Review	"Deliverance"
Kenyon Review	"There Together Is Enough"
Narrative	"Dear Lord if there is good in store"
Orion	"Given Names"
The Southern Review	"Reparation"
ZYZZYVA	"To See It"

On this journey with words, I am immensely grateful for my teachers, writers, and co-travelers at Stanford University, Indiana University, Bread Loaf Writers' Conference, Sewanee Writers' Conference, Community of Writers, Tin House Writers Workshop, Napa Valley Writers Workshop, Palm Beach Poetry Festival, Vermont Studio Center, Tasajillo Residency, and Rutgers Institute for Global Racial Justice.

Thank you Keetje, Craig, and Marcus for championing these poems—your support means more than you know. My enduring gratitude also to Poet's Table (San Francisco and Chicago), for their presence in community; to 32 Poems' many interviewees who have shaped me as a writer and kept conversations going. And oceans-deep gratitude to all my letter writers—Ryan, Ryan, Ross, Airin, Jay, Nicole, JT—who have buoyed me well over a decade.

Ryan, Jill, Enzo—thank you for getting me in the water. Every day is better with my belly on the Pacific. And to the Lasses—my overflowing thanks for all the nights at my favorite place—they let the lines come.

Still, these poems wouldn't have seen the light of day were it not for David and Lisa—such incredible readers and friends. Nor would this collection have been possible without the belief of Ross, Noah, and the Bull City team. I'm honored to join your press family.

Gratitude, too, to our Good Sam family who have helped sustain my own. And my own, for whom I have no words. My heart is your heart.

And finally, for the ocean, and the spirit moving over the waters—my eternal awe and thanksgiving. You have been there from the beginning.

ABOUT THE AUTHOR

CATE LYCURGUS's poetry has appeared in *Best American Poetry*, *The American Poetry Review*, *Ploughshares*, *Orion*, and elsewhere. She interviews for *32 Poems* and teaches professional writing in San Jose, California.